中英双语版

企鹅经典 名人大发现

苏斯博士

[美] 珍妮特·B. 帕斯卡尔（Janet B.Pascal）◎著 [美] 南希·哈里森（Nancy Harrison）◎绘 王芬芬◎译

Who Was Dr. Seuss?

U0870819

湖南科学技术出版社 小博集

·长沙·

著作权合同登记号：字18-2024-197

图书在版编目（CIP）数据

名人大发现．苏斯博士：汉英对照 /（美）珍妮特·B. 帕斯卡尔（Janet B. Pascal）著；王芬芬译；（美）南希·哈里森（Nancy Harrison）绘. -- 长沙：湖南科学技术出版社，2025. 1. --（企鹅经典）.
ISBN 978-7-5710-3275-3

Ⅰ. H319. 4

中国国家版本馆CIP数据核字第20243D3L55号

上架建议：科普读物

QI'E JINGDIAN · MINGREN DA FAXIAN：ZHONG-YING SHUANGYU BAN SUSI BOSHI

企鹅经典·名人大发现：中英双语版　苏斯博士

著　　者：［美］珍妮特·B. 帕斯卡尔（Janet B. Pascal）
绘　　者：［美］南希·哈里森（Nancy Harrison）
译　　者：王芬芬
出 版 人：潘晓山
责任编辑：刘　竞
策划出品：李　炜　张苗苗　文赛峰
策划编辑：马　瑄
特约编辑：杜佳美
营销编辑：付　佳　杨　朔　周晓茜
装帧设计：利　锐
内文排版：金锋工作室
出　　版：湖南科学技术出版社
（湖南省长沙市芙蓉中路416号　邮编：410008）
网　　址：www.hnstp.com
印　　刷：三河市航远印刷有限公司
经　　销：新华书店
开　　本：875 mm × 1230 mm 1/32
字　　数：96千字
印　　张：5
版　　次：2025年1月第1版
印　　次：2025年1月第1次印刷
书　　号：ISBN 978-7-5710-3275-3
定　　价：22.00元

若有质量问题，请致电质量监督电话：010-59096394　　团购电话：010-59320018

目 录

Contents

谁是苏斯博士？

1985 年，普林斯顿大学授予六人荣誉博士学位。只有为世界做出杰出贡献的人才能获此殊荣。其中一人最受学生们关注。一个又高又瘦、花白胡子的男子起身时，学生们迅速站立。“我是萨姆，”他们高喊着，“我是萨姆。”然后凭着记忆，朗诵出整本《绿鸡蛋和火腿》。学

生们用这种特殊的方式表明西奥多·盖泽尔——大名鼎鼎的苏斯博士——写的书，对他们意义非凡。

米歇尔·鲁宾逊是当年普林斯顿大学这些学生中的一员。若干年后，她嫁给了贝拉克·奥巴马，并成为美国第一夫人。2010年，她选了苏斯博士的另一本书《戴帽子的猫》，给美国的孩子们朗读。第一夫人知道，过去为初级读者编写的书大部分严肃枯燥。但苏斯博士的书韵律十足、朗朗上口，角色荒诞古怪，比如戴帽子的猫、霍顿和格林奇。孩子们的学习阅读从此不一样了。

第一章

愚蠢的机器

西奥多·苏斯·盖泽尔，1904年3月2日出生于马萨诸塞州的斯普林菲尔德。当地到处是生产汽车、枪支、自行车、轮胎和玩具的工厂。其中有一家泰德[①]的祖父创办的啤酒厂，叫“卡姆巴克和盖泽尔”。后来啤酒厂由泰德的父亲接管。他们酿造的啤酒深受斯普林菲尔德人喜欢，故他们的生意被戏称为“来狂饮吧”。

泰德成长在一个喜欢玩文字游戏的家庭。母亲家有一间面包房。母亲小时候就会编韵文介绍不同口味的馅饼。后来，她又用这些韵文当摇篮曲哄孩子入睡。所以泰德相信自己之所以热爱韵文，是因为记忆中的那些关于馅饼的押韵诗歌。

① 泰德：泰德是西奥多的昵称。

他姐姐比他大两岁，叫玛格丽特。但她给自己取了个小名“玛尼·梅卡丁丁·盖伊。”

父亲也叫西奥多，他喜欢在闲暇时光琢磨一些怪异复杂的发明。其中泰德最喜欢“丝袜背缝错误检测镜”这个小发明。

小泰德喜欢逛动物园。因为他父亲帮忙管理动物园，所以他可以享受一些特殊待遇。他有时说："我可以进笼子里和小狮子、小老虎在一起，并且我时不时就会被咬一口。"（众所周知他讲故事喜欢夸大其词。）

从动物园回去后，泰德会急忙回家，在卧室墙上画动物。但他画的动物与现实中看见的不一样，因此他给这些动物取了名字。他妈妈最喜欢的是一只长着九英尺[①]长的耳朵的怪物。他给它取名“韦恩”。

① 英尺：英美制长度单位，1 英尺≈0.305 米。

和斯普林菲尔德里的很多人一样，盖泽尔一家是德国移民。泰德从小就会说德语和英语。1914 年，第一次世界大战在欧洲爆发。众多国家对德国开战。美国没有参战（1917 年之前）。但是德国人在美国越来越不受欢迎。

在学校，德裔美国孩子经常被欺凌。有时泰德也会被扔石头。盖泽尔一家想方设法证明他们热爱美国。泰德学校的童子军举办了一场比赛，看谁能卖出最多的战

争债券——以此帮助政府支持战事。泰德祖父购买了价值一千美元的债券，因此泰德成为赢家之一。

颁奖典礼上，前总统西奥多·罗斯福颁发了奖牌。但由于童子军工作人员的失误，出现了十个赢家，而罗斯福只有九块奖牌。奖牌发完了，泰德还孤零零地站在舞台上。罗斯福吼道："这个小男孩在这里干吗？"没有人出面解释泰德也是赢家。泰德只得灰溜溜地下去了。

从那以后，泰德总是在人前抬不起头。甚至成名后，他也拒绝发表演讲。有一次他试着参加电视台脱口秀，但是却被吓得一个字也说不出来。

1918 年第一次世界大战结束，泰德家面临新问题。1920 年初，美国开始实行禁酒令。这意味着制造和销售酒——包括啤酒，是违法的。啤酒厂不得不关闭，泰德的爸爸失业了。一家人还有积蓄可以生活下去。但失去啤酒厂是一个沉重的打击。积蓄也越用越少，这时泰德即将高中毕业。但重视教育的盖泽尔家，无论如何也会确保有足够的钱让泰德上大学。

泰德对学业从不用心。大部分时间他都在给校报写笑话。他唯一感兴趣的是英语课。

泰德的英语老师曾就读于新罕布什尔州的达特茅斯学院。泰德非常喜欢达特茅斯学院，便决定也去那里。

禁酒令

1920 年，美国通过被称为禁酒令的第十八号修正案，从此，在美国生产或销售酒是违法的。激进分子认为喝酒毁了人们的生活。但禁酒令并不成功。像黑手党这样的犯罪集团因走私酒变得更嚣张。像阿尔·卡彭这样的黑帮变成了人民英雄。尽管会触犯法律，但大多数人还是继续喝酒。许多城市都有一个“地下酒吧”，只要知道口令或敲门动作，就可以去那里买酒。

该修正案对盖泽尔家这样以卖酒为生的人，无疑是沉重一击。（泰德永远不会忘记这对他的家庭造成的影响。他的许多早期漫画作品都是讽刺禁酒令的。）以酿酒厂闻名的城市突然失去了最重要的生意，还有与酒相关的税收和就业机会。一些啤酒厂试图靠卖汽水为生。还有一些转为卖葡萄汁或麦芽糖浆。厂家会“用心良苦”地告诉大家哪些是不能做的，以确保果汁或糖浆不会转化成酒精。到了20世纪30年代，禁酒令显然是失败的。1933年，富兰克林·罗斯福总统签署了一项法律，禁酒令得以终止。然后罗斯福总统说：“我想现在正是喝啤酒的好时机。”

第二章

一头会飞的奶牛

泰德喜欢达特茅斯学院，该学校坐落在绿色的乡村，周围有很多漂亮的古建筑。他在那里结交了很多终生好友。到校后不久，他就知道了学校的幽默杂志——《杰克南瓜灯》，大家将它戏称为《杰克灯》。他梦想着能到该杂志社工作，所以一有时间就待在办公室。社员们总是大清早就看见他趴在打字机前，沉沉地睡着。

很快他就被选入该社工作，大三结束时，升为总编辑。同学们喜欢他的故事和绘画，他也成了达特茅斯学院的重要人物。即便如此，同学却都说他是“最不可能成功的人”。因为泰德似乎从不认真对待某事。

毕业前一个月，泰德搞了一次聚会。客人们共饮了一瓶杜松子酒。之后两个男生在屋顶上胡闹，泰德的房东报了警。禁酒令期间，喝杜松子酒是违法的，因此泰德惹上了大麻烦。

作为惩罚，他被禁止给

《杰克灯》写稿。但是他想到了解决办法。他用假名投稿。他用过一些搞笑的名字，比如欧拉拉麦卡蒂和西奥尔塞盖〔把盖泽尔（Geisel）倒过来拼写就是尔塞盖（Lesieg）〕。现在他开始用中间名苏斯。

在达特茅斯学院，泰德把所有时间都花在《杰克灯》杂志上。他的成绩不好。父亲担心他毕业后找不到工作。但泰德让父亲不要为此担忧。因为他即将去牛津大学，这是英国的一所名校。他还说自己拿到了奖学金！父亲非常激动，把此事告诉了当地报社。第二天，泰德便成了新闻人物。

可问题是，虽然泰德确实申请了牛津大学，但并未拿到奖学金，只是希望能拿到。父亲是一

个傲气的人，因为已经把泰德将去牛津大学深造的消息传出去了，所以他决定支付儿子的上学费用。1925 年夏天，泰德登上一艘蒸汽船，长途跋涉去了英国。

泰德从未真正适应牛津大学。这是一所有八百年历史的学校，学生们看起来都严肃正经。他觉得课程枯燥，虽然尽力认真听讲做笔记，但总是开小差，在本子上乱涂乱画。他的笔

记本里面全是长着风车尾巴的鸡，走钢丝的狗和长翅膀的奶牛。

海伦·帕尔默，也是美国人，在牛津大学学习，将来想当老师。一天，她站在泰德身后看他画什么。

“这是一头会飞的奶牛！”她说。

海伦说泰德的画作风格独特。她认为他可以当插画师。海伦的这番话改变了泰德的命运。他意识到自己不喜欢教书，不喜欢写小说，只想一直画乱七八糟的动物。之后，泰德整天和海伦在一起。一天，泰德向海伦求婚，她答应了。但因为没有钱，两人暂时还不能成婚。

海伦从牛津大学毕业后，在新泽西州一所学校当老师。泰德退学了，回到马萨诸塞州斯普林菲尔德父母家。他知道自己这一生想做什么，但眼下必须搞清楚如何靠画画谋生。

第三章

野兽和怪物们

回到父母家后，泰德一心画漫画、写幽默文章，把作品寄给他能想到的纽约的各种杂志、大学朋友和广告商。但除了海伦，大家都不喜欢会飞的奶牛和跳舞的狗。

之后一家著名杂志《周六晚邮报》刊登了他的一幅漫画。泰德画的是两个撑着阳伞的优雅游客，坐在两匹温顺的骆驼身上，想象着自己是勇敢的探险者。他在画作上简单署名“苏斯”。

《周六晚邮报》支付给他二十五美元。即便在 1927 年，这也不是一笔大钱，但够支付一个月房租。而且泰德认为这足以证明他可以画插画谋生。于是他搬到纽约城。但在有固定收入之前，他还是无法迎娶海伦。泰

德和达特茅斯学院的一个朋友合住在一套公寓。租金便宜但屋内很脏。每晚睡觉前，他们不得不抄起棍子赶老鼠。

泰德的这个室友认识一个在幽默杂志《法官》工作的人。经他介绍，杂志社让泰德去上班。他成了一个作家兼画家，且可以获得薪水。

现在他有能力迎娶海伦了。不过因为姐姐玛尼快生孩子了，而泰德希望全家人都能来参加他的婚礼，于是改了结婚日期。泰德的外甥女佩吉生于 1927 年 11 月 1 日。11 月 29 日，泰德和海伦在海伦父母家客厅完婚。

泰德在《法官》杂志大受欢迎。他开始写专栏《野兽和怪物们》，介绍他那些古怪有趣的动物。他署名“苏斯博士”，加上“博士”是因为他当初从哈佛大学退学未获得博士学位的事令父亲失望了。

不幸的是，《法官》杂志出现了资金问题。总是没有足够的现金发工资。在《法官》杂志登广告的企业没有现金，便用样品支付广告费。于是这些样品成了员工工资。所以泰德经常领到几盒剃须膏或者几箱饮料。有一次他还收到一千八百七十二个指甲钳。这导致他无法支付每天的生活费。

1928 年，好运突然降临。这始于一款流行的杀虫剂“一扫净”。有空调之前，在夏天人们总是敞开窗户让凉风吹进来，这也导致屋里到处都是小飞虫。于是泰德就想，对古代的骑士们来说，夏季一定很难熬。屋内有飞虫就够难受了——万一龙飞进来咬人怎么办呢？

于是他画了一幅漫画，画的是一个身披盔甲的骑士因为屋内有一条飞龙而睡不着觉。漫画配文是：“该死的，我刚用“一扫净”喷洒了整个城堡，又来了一条龙。”

“一扫净”公司一个广告主管的妻子在美容院做美容时，碰巧看见了杂志上的这幅漫画。她非常喜欢这幅漫画，就叫他丈夫雇泰德为“一扫净”画广告。

泰德画人们被飞虫叮咬时的滑稽画面。这成了历史上最成功的广告策划之一。

如今几乎没人还记得泰德创造的那句广告口号：“快，亨利，拿‘一扫净’！”但是 20 世纪 20 年代末到 50 年代，这句广告尽人皆知。喜剧演员经常引用这句广

告，它还被唱进了流行音乐。“一扫净”杀虫剂销量飙升。苏斯博士的画也变得有名。

“一扫净”以每年一万两千美元的高薪聘用泰德——在当时这可是一大笔钱。第二年，股票市场崩盘，美国陷入经济大萧条。国内百姓失去工作、贫困饥饿。但多亏了“一扫净”，泰德存了很多钱。

有了钱后，他和海伦开始举办宴会。他们的社交生活丰富多彩，泰德也成了朋友圈里尽人皆知的恶作剧高手。有一次他溜进厨房，把一颗硕大的塑料珍珠塞进即将端上桌的牡蛎肚子里。还有一次，他把果冻和金鱼倒进朋友的浴缸里。

1931 年，泰德的母亲去世，享年五十二岁。她的早逝令泰德深受打击。但所幸她见证了泰德的第一次大成功。

“一扫净”公司让泰德经济上得到保障，但是有一个问题：他不想把所有时间都花在为“一扫净”公司画广告上。但他的合同不允许他做其他大部分事情。多年后他写道：“我想，之所以创作儿童书籍，是因为我非常了解儿童。”其实并非如此。事实上，给童书画插画是合同中允许他做的为数不多的事情之一。

组约公寓

盖泽尔夫妇在曼哈顿的第一套公寓，隔街与一个马厩相望。很快他们就搬到了一套条件更好的公寓中。他家的电话号码与附近一家鱼店的电话号码就差了一个数字，所以他们经常接到想买鱼的顾客打来的电话。泰德并不会说他们拨错了号码，而是把顾客要的鱼画在纸上并送到鱼店去。当时并非人人都觉得好笑，但是想想，那些画作现在可是价值不菲啊！

第四章

我在桑树街看见的

维京图书的一个编辑看见了“一扫净”杀虫剂的广告，于是聘用泰德给一本小学生错误集画插画。于是泰德便给一些犯低级错误的引文配图，比如“本杰明·富兰克林把猫毛往后捋，发明了电”。这本书 1931 年出版。令泰德惊讶的是，此书大受欢迎——维京图书续签了合同，要他创作续集。

不久，泰德意识到如果自己写书，自己画插画，可以赚更多钱，于是便着手给自己的第一本书寻找最佳主题。

1936 年，泰德和海伦乘船去欧洲。在回来的船上，他在笔记本上乱涂乱画，构思插画书——写下了“一匹笨马和一辆马车”和“飞猫拉维京船”这些想法，但似乎都行不通。同时，他又被轮船发动机轰隆隆的噪声吵得快疯了。他便给图片添文字。突然他反复念着：“这个故事无人能及。这是我在桑树街看见的。”

他写的故事是这样的。一个小男孩沿着桑树街——泰德家乡的一条主街——步行回家，寻找着趣事，以便回家告诉爸爸。可他只看见“一匹普通的马和一辆马车”。回到家时，他把马和马车变成了由几头蓝色大象和一个铜管乐队组成的巡游马戏团。

苏斯博士的书韵味十足，且押韵自然，以至于人们觉得这很容易创作。但其实他付出了很多辛苦。“我知道我的故事看起来二十八秒就可以全部写完，”他解释，“但其实每一个字都颇费脑筋。”创作一本图画书，他可能要撕掉几百上千页稿纸。

最后，泰德很满意《桑树街漫游记》。他把这本书寄给出版商，但他们都婉拒了它。大部分编辑认为这样的作品太另类了，韵文粗糙愚蠢。最糟糕的是这本书没有道德意义，不能帮助儿童端正品行。泰德愤怒地呐喊：“让孩子开心阅读，而不是被灌输道理，这有何错?”

在正要放弃之际，泰德遇见了另一个达特茅斯学院的朋友马歇尔·麦克林托克。马歇尔·麦克林托克当天刚成为先锋出版社的儿童图书编辑。该出版社经常发表“另类”作品。他们对泰德的这本书非常满意并同意发表。泰德对马歇尔·麦克林托克感激不尽，并用麦克林托克儿子的名字“马尔科”给书中主角命名。

第五章

树上的大象

评论家们很喜欢《桑树街漫游记》，这本书销量火爆，成了儿童畅销书。但经济大萧条期间，老百姓没有多少钱能用来买儿童书。为了生存，泰德不得不继续画广告插画。他无法分辨自己到底是真正的作者还是“卑微的广告商”。

他第二本书的灵感源自他最喜欢的一样东西——帽子。他和海伦喜欢去旅游。每到一个地方，他都会买帽子，要么是秘鲁的渔夫帽，要么是帅气的欧洲头盔。有时写作没有思路，他就会戴上一顶帽子当成“思考帽”。一天，泰德创造了一顶最有名的帽子，并把帽子戴在了一只猫的头上，写出了《巴塞洛缪·库宾斯的五百顶帽子》。

泰德和海伦最近得知他们无法拥有自己的孩子。后来，泰德说反正他也不想要孩子，因为孩子会让他紧张。“你们有孩子，我就让你们的孩子开心。”他总是这样跟人们说。但他的外甥女

相信，他其实很想有一个自己的孩子。

面对一些不好的事情，他总是有自己的处理方式。他创造了一个女儿叫“珍珠菊”，并为她写了一本新书。他和海伦有时会把珍珠菊连同其他想象出来的孩子，比如诺弗尔、威克沙姆和斯纳德，写进圣诞贺卡里。

出版了两本儿童书后，苏斯博士声名鹊起。泰德经常用德语写自己的名“佐斯”，但大部分读者念成“苏斯”。泰德喜欢这个名字，因为它和《鹅妈妈童谣》

（*Mother Goose*）中的 Goose 押韵，所以他也开始叫自己“苏斯”。

比先锋更大的一家出版社“兰登书屋”，对苏斯博士的作品很感兴趣。“兰登书屋”社长贝内特·瑟夫答应出版泰德写的任何作品。这让泰德如何拒绝呢？尽管不舍得离开先锋出版社的朋友们，但他也很爱“兰登书屋”。他余生都在这家出版社发行自己的作品。多年来，他和那里很多同事成了好朋友。

他为“兰登书屋”写的第一本书并不尽如人意。《七公主格蒂瓦斯》是写给成年人的，且里面尽是裸体女子的图片。泰德并不擅长写这类作品，贝内特·瑟夫也认为这本书写得不好，但仍信守承诺，随泰德之意出版了这本书。这本书彻底搞砸了。泰德只得继续创作儿童文学。

1939 的某天（他是这么说的），泰德没有关窗户。放在窗外的涂鸦画被风吹得打转。他回来时看见一幅大象的画压在一棵大树的画上面。大象怎么在树上呢？在孵蛋吗？泰德给大象取名霍顿，但他想不出大象发生了什么事。

“我很难过，”海伦对朋友说，“泰德在故事中写大象爬上了一棵树，但他不知道如何让它下来。”最后还是海伦想到了一个结局。霍顿孵出了一头会飞的象，就如她曾在泰德的本子上见到的会飞的奶牛。

泰德喜欢《霍顿孵蛋》这本书，胜过他写的其他书。他告诉编辑这是他写过的最有趣的儿童故事。大家都喜欢这个故事。大象霍顿一直是苏斯博士创作的角色里最受欢迎的一个。

但是 1940 年此书出版时，泰德已经不再想着会飞的大象了。他对周遭世界感到担忧和不悦。第二次世界大战在欧洲爆发。他父母的故乡德国被阿道夫 · 希特勒和纳粹控制。希特勒想统领整个欧洲。大部分美国人希望美国不要卷入战争，但泰德不这么想。尽管他讨厌战争，但是必须阻止纳粹。如果他的搞笑漫画可以说服人们购买“一扫净”杀虫剂，那么是否也可以说服人们攻打希特勒呢？于是泰德转身投入战争，七年未写过儿童书籍。

第六章

大兵斯纳福

泰德开始画政治类漫画，讽刺那些认为美国不应该参战的人。他把这些人画成不顾周围危险，把头埋在沙子里的鸵鸟。

1941 年 12 月 7 日，德国盟军日本轰炸位于夏威夷的珍珠港，美国参战。这时泰德感觉单画漫画还不够。

可他已三十七岁，过了当兵的年龄，不过仍旧报了名。其实军队十分清楚这样一个柔弱笨拙、手无缚鸡之力的画家最适合做什么。他被送往加利福尼亚的好莱坞，拍摄用来训练新兵的电影。

泰德对拍电影一窍不通，但他知道如何吸引人们的兴趣。他协助创作了《大兵斯纳福》动画片。大兵斯纳福是一个懒惰粗心、净做错事的士兵。斯纳福（SNAFU）代表“情况正常，一切搞砸（Situation Normal, All Fouled Up）”。《大兵斯纳福》教育士兵们什么事不能做。

后来，泰德获得晋升，转为制作人，拍摄现实生活的影片。他协助创作了两部有关战争胜利后，美国应该在德国和日本做什么的电影。改编后两部电影都获得了奥斯卡奖。但现在完全没人记得了。

获得两项奥斯卡奖后，泰德认为自己也许可以从写书转为制作电影，但很快就改变了想法。因为他发现战后的世界既充满希望也暗藏危险。所以他认为没有比写儿童书籍更重要的事。“后代们必须成长得比我们更睿智。”他写道。

优先捍卫美国!

战争的问题

1941 年初，百分之八十的美国人反对美国加入对德之战。这些人被称为隔绝分子，他们认为美洲和欧洲隔了整整一个大洋，离欧洲的麻烦十万八千里远。他们认为美国的职责就是保护自己。

但是泰德并不认为自己与欧洲的战事隔绝。他说：“巴黎被纳粹轰隆隆的坦克占领时……我无法安心画大象霍顿。”在他的政治讽刺漫画中，泰德尽力表现出世界各国的紧密关联。在一幅漫画中，他画山姆大叔在欢快沐浴。山姆大叔心想：“家里这口旧浴缸非常安全。”那是因为他闭上了双眼，所以没看见浴缸里有一条鲨鱼、一只鳄鱼和一只毒虫正要大口吃掉他。

第七章

一只麋鹿、一个奇怪的小动物和无名氏

玛尼

第二次世界大战结束时，姐姐玛尼去世，泰德转喜为悲。他和姐姐因一次家庭争吵早已不相往来。还没和好她就去世了，这令泰德悲痛万分，以至于他余生都在避免谈起姐姐。

战争结束后，泰德和海伦决定留在加利福尼亚。他们在太平洋海岸加利福尼亚一个漂亮的海滨城镇拉霍亚外面的山上，买了一座老旧的瞭望塔。这座塔一直空着，成了一些年轻情侣最爱的聚会场所。所以墙上刻满了姓名首字母的缩写。盖泽尔夫妇搬进来住之后，一些情侣还是会试图进来。

泰德在战后写的第一批书，其中一本叫《慷慨大方的麋鹿》。麋鹿十分友善，任由其他动物欺负它。故事结尾处，泰德问读者们："那么，如果你被欺负了，你会怎

么做?”泰德的很多书都是以这种提问的方式结尾。他希望孩子们喜欢他的故事，但也想引导孩子们独立思考。

泰德开始每年出版一两本书。每一本都趣味十足、创新独特，且故事各不相同，所以人们总是问他灵感源自何处，他说他一般从乱涂乱画开始。“我会画两只动物。如果它们互相撕咬，这将是一个好故事。”过了一段时间，他厌倦了回答这个问题，于是说灵感源自一个叫

“于贝尔·格雷奇”的小镇居民。“每年夏天的8月4日，我都会去那里维修布谷鸟钟。”从那以后，谁问他——即便约翰·菲茨杰拉德·肯尼迪总统的夫人杰奎琳问，他都是这样回答。

他的部分灵感源于现实世界。1953 年，泰德和海伦受《生活》杂志委派，到日本了解该国如何应对战后事宜。泰德对日本人怀有复杂的情感。在战争期间画的漫画中，他把日本人甚至美国人，都画成坏人。

但他跟日本的老师和学生交流时，克服了这种偏见。他看见日本人正努力尊重每个人的重要性，并为了共同利益通力合作。

回到工作室，泰德对在日本了解到的情况进行了一番探讨。他又想到了自己最爱的角色——大象霍顿，在《霍顿与无名氏》一书中，霍顿必须证明无名镇的存在来挽救这个小世界。要成功，只有让每一个无名氏，甚至包括最小最懒的那个，一起合作。为了无名氏，霍顿甘愿冒一切风险，因为“不管多么小，每一个人都值得存在”。泰德把这本书献给了一个日本朋友。

《霍顿与无名氏》出版时，泰德的生活被个人烦心事占据。海伦身患重病。她无法自主呼吸，不得不被装进一个铁肺——一个包裹着她大部分躯干的大金属箱子——里。在医院里，泰德在她身边坐了好几个小时。海伦回到家后，泰德在家里装上镜子，方便海伦看在外面玩耍的狗狗。

泰德凡事都依赖海伦。海伦会给他写的书出主意，打理他的生活。没有海伦，泰德甚至不知道如何平衡收支。

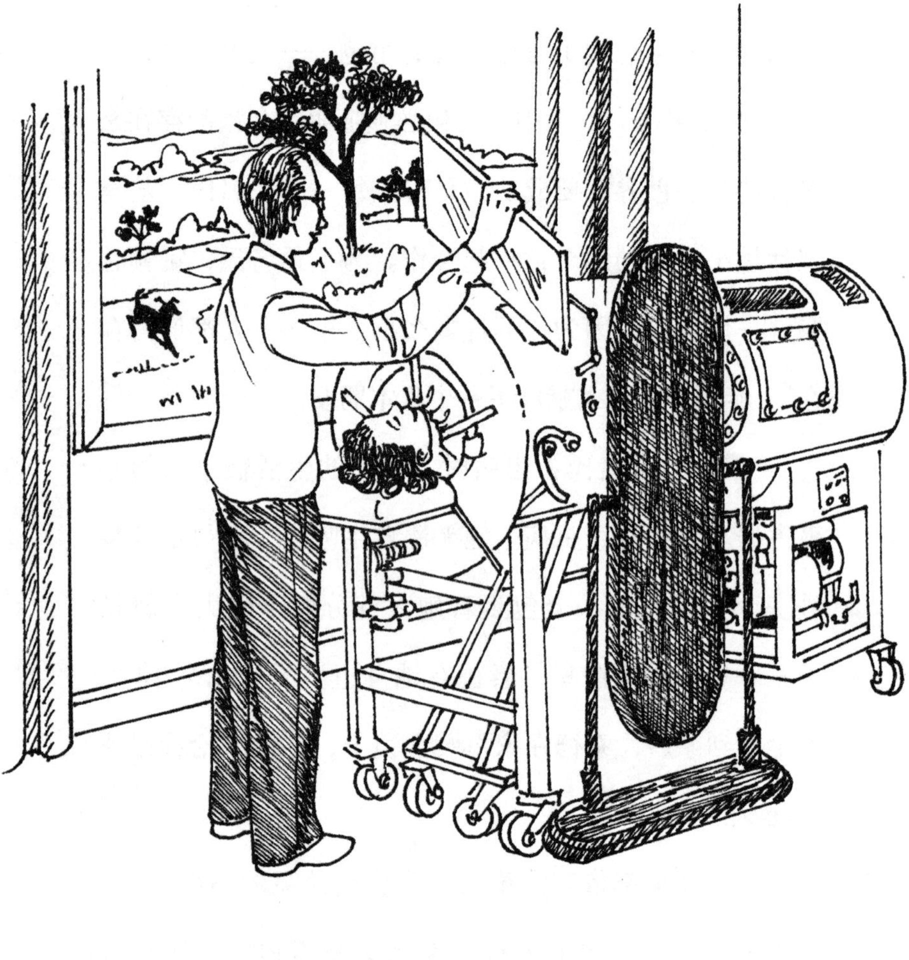

令医生惊讶的是，海伦几乎痊愈了。1955 年 5 月，

她还和泰德一起回到达特茅斯学院，见证他获得荣誉博

士学位。多年前，他没有获得牛津大学博士学位，令父亲失望了，现在弥补了这一点。他扬言自己现在不只是“苏斯博士”，还是“博士苏斯博士”。

第一个“NERD”

泰德喜欢创作如“thneed[①]”和“Sala-Ma-Goo[②]”这样的词语。其中一本书里的一个词就成了英语语言中的一个通用词。苏斯博士是第一个使用“NERD”这个单词的，它出现在1959年出版的《如果我经营动物园》书里。小杰拉尔德·麦格鲁计划“航海去卡特罗，带回一个NERD（奇怪的小动物）”。不知为何，不到一年时间，底特律的青少年们都在用“NERD”来代表“奇怪的小动物”，很快这个新词就传遍了全国。

① Thneed，也称塑料假城，是《老雷斯的故事》里一个由塑料组成的小镇，所有的景观、食物都是塑料制品。

② Sala-Ma-Goo，沙拉－玛－咕岛，是《乌龟耶尔特及其他故事》里创造的一个小岛名。

第八章

戴帽子的猫来了

1954年，广受欢迎的《生活》周刊杂志刊登了一篇文章，质问为何美国儿童在学习阅读时会遇到这么多困难。是因为初级阅读者的读物太枯燥了吗？老师们认为儿童是通过反复看同样的单词来学习阅读的。所以初级读物应该使用短句来重复同一件事。聪明的孩子们怎么可能愿意看这种枯燥的书呢？假如像苏斯博士那样的人写一本初级读物，或许孩子们会愿意看。

泰德的一个朋友威廉·斯波尔丁，在霍顿·米夫林出版社上班。他看见了这篇文章并对泰德说："给我写一个一年级学生看了舍不得放下的故事！"泰德愿意一试。兰登书屋和霍顿·米夫林达成协议。霍顿·米夫林出版社把书卖给学校和图书馆，兰登书屋则卖给书商。

威廉·斯波尔丁给了泰德一张单词表，上面有大部分一年级学生都认识的大约三百个单词。他只能从中使用大约二百二十五个单词来创作。泰德本以为自己不费心思就能很快写出一个小故事——但很快他就发现这是

不可能的。他每次想到了一个故事点子，却发现想用的词不在这张单词表上面。他花了一年多时间尝试，但是都失败了。最终他决定“再读一遍这张单词表，如果能找到两个押韵的词，那就是我要创作的书籍内容”。他找到了——“猫”和“帽子”[①]——《戴帽子的猫》由此而生。

---

① 猫（cat）和帽子（hat），这两个英语单词的发音押韵。

《戴帽子的猫》于 1957 年出版。很多老师都不喜欢这本书。他们认为这本书看起来像图画书，不严肃正统。一些图书管理员把它藏起来，不让孩子们找到。负责学校和图书馆销售的霍顿·米夫林出版社，没卖出几本。

但是孩子们喜欢《戴帽子的猫》。他们互相谈论书里面的内容，还在朋友间相互传阅这本书。这些书一上架，就被买走了，不断有人来买它。三年内，这本书卖

出一百多万册。泰德说："在我自己写的书里面，这本书是最令我骄傲的……"

而在兰登书屋，本内特·瑟夫的妻子菲利斯认为《戴帽子的猫》只是个开始。她想出版一整套这类书——这种只用少量单词编写，但又趣味十足，孩子们都真正喜欢看的书。她说服丈夫让她在兰登书屋成立一家新的子品牌出版公司，由菲利斯、泰德和海伦来经营，名叫"初级读物"公司，给初级读者出版苏斯博士和其他人写的书。

很快，“初级读物”公司轰动一时。兰登书屋也因此成为美国最大的儿童书籍出版商。泰德很高兴出版在部队里结识的老友写的书，比如P.D.伊士曼写的《你是我妈妈吗？》和《快跑，狗狗。快跑！》。他还出版了先锋出版社总编马歇尔·麦克林托克的书，此人早几年曾是泰德的引路人。另外泰德还发现并出版了斯坦和简·博丹所写的“贝贝熊”系列书籍。

本内特·瑟夫对“初级读物”公司作者们使用的单词表很感兴趣。“如果只用三百个单词来写一本书就这么难，”他问，“那么用更少的单词呢？”他跟泰德赌五十美元，说泰德只用五十个单词写不出一本书。结果本内特·瑟夫赌输了，泰德写出了配有插画的《绿鸡蛋和火腿》，刚好五十个单词。这本书一直是他最受欢迎的书，还一直是儿童畅销书第四名。

婴儿潮一代

“初级读物”公司成立的时机刚刚好。第二次世界大战结束后，美国家庭开始大量生育。到1957年，刚开始学习阅读的孩子比以前任何时候都多。同时，美国越来越害怕苏联——一个共产主义国家联盟。人们担心这些国家的学校更善于将孩子培养成科学家和发明家。所以1958年，美国政府开始给学校和图书馆投钱。其中一部分钱被用来购买书籍，比如苏斯博士初级读物系列。

第九章

格林奇、乌龟耶尔特和史尼奇

1957 年，因为《戴帽子的猫》这本书，泰德成了明星作家，也当上了自己出版社的老板。这还不够，一年后，他又创作了“格林奇”。

泰德喜欢暗示“格林奇”是苏斯博士自己。他甚至有一块写着“格林奇”的牌照。至于这个名字的由来，他说：“我只是先画了一个人，然后盯着看，结果就清楚了他是谁。”

《格林奇偷走圣诞节》刚一出版，就风靡一时。几年后，泰德接到老朋友查克·琼斯的电话。他现在是著名的动画片制作者，创作了《哔哔鸟和笨狼怀尔》。他想把“格林奇”搬上电视屏幕。泰德有点担心这个提议，但他信任琼斯。甚至同意他把“格林奇”变成绿色的。（书里的“格林奇”有黑白相间的毛发和粉色的眼睛。）1966年《圣诞怪杰》登上电视，从此便成了节日新宠。

佩吉

泰德和海伦终于过上了自己想要的生活。他们有足够的钱，泰德无须再去接广告了。海伦则热衷于打理好生活的方方面面，让泰德可以整天写写画画。他们没有生育小孩，但和泰德的外甥女佩吉关系密切。

佩吉还是小宝宝时，泰德就喜欢逗她玩。即便他和玛尼关系搞僵不说话后，他依然和佩吉保持联系。佩吉二十几岁时搬去了加利福尼亚。她在盖泽尔夫妇的塔楼里住了一段时间，还在那儿结婚生子。她儿子叫泰迪，

简直是另一个泰德，就像是盖泽尔夫妇的外孙。他像泰德一样安静平和、温文尔雅，也想当画家。泰迪是少数几个在泰德写作时被允许进入他书房的人。

接下来十年间，泰德写了十二本书，包括经典书籍《戴帽子的猫》《回来》《一条鱼两条鱼红色鱼蓝色鱼》和《在爸爸身上跳啊跳》。

泰德的书都非常有趣，但同时引人深思。《乌龟耶尔特及其他故事》讲述的是一个欺负周围人的暴君和一只勇敢站出来制止他的普通小乌龟的故事。泰德以希特勒为原型创作了“耶尔特”，本来担心人们无法接受。但实际上，人们唯一的问题是小乌龟为何会打嗝。“因为儿童书里，从未有角色打嗝啊。”泰德这样解释。

另一本对他意义重大的书是《史尼奇及其他故事》。20世纪60年代初，黑人努力争取公民权。在这本书里面，泰德描写了肚皮上有星星的史尼奇和没有星星的史尼奇之间的矛盾。这个故事表明泰德认为：人们因为外貌不同而互相憎恨是非常愚蠢的。

创作这些书籍是非常辛苦的。泰德一周七天，每天八小时坐在书桌前。他说当他把自己逼入绝境时，作品写得最好——“似乎没有办法结束这本书”——不得不自己想办法结束。

每当这时，海伦就得顾及泰德的心情。她解释：“每本书结束前两周，他都会认为书里的内容写得都不好……”这时她就得做他的思想工作，让他忘掉这一切。

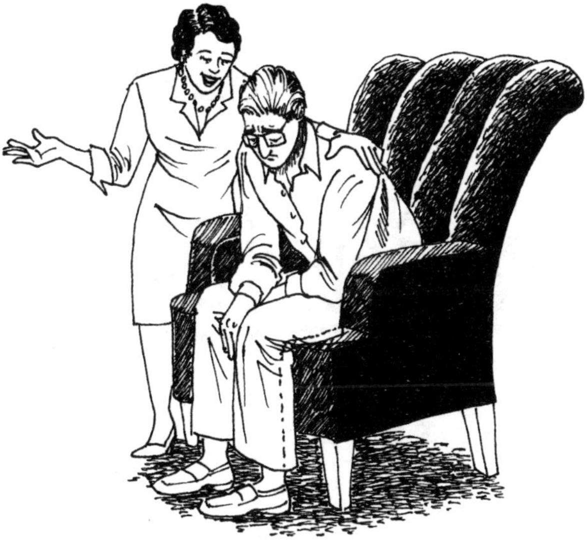

每写完一本书，他都会心情糟糕。他总是担心：“我再也不写了，我没思路了，写不出来了。”然后看到那些涂鸦画，他的脑瓜子又转起来了，他又开心了。

泰德一生一直以工作为中心，但有时也会休息。他和海伦乐此不疲地环游世界。他们去墨西哥看象鼻海豹，去秘鲁帮着寻找木乃伊，还去了澳大利亚、非洲和夏威夷。

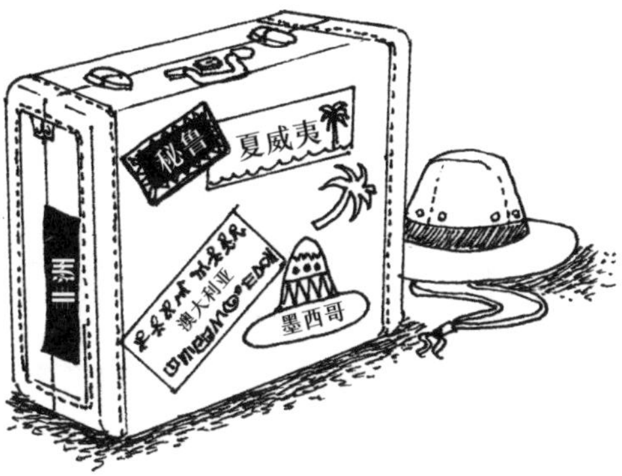

“格林奇”用汉语怎么说?

圣诞怪杰

起初，苏斯博士的书在美国以外的国家并不出名。英国人觉得他的书风格过于“美国化”——庸俗粗野，很多俚语表达。而且因为苏斯博士多用韵文和自创的单词，导致翻译困难，所以要把他的书推广到其他国家非常难。但还是有睿智的翻译员做出了尝试。不久，苏斯博士的名声享誉全球。作品被译成二十多种语言，包括汉语、瑞典语、西班牙语、希伯来语、毛利语、拉丁语、日语、希腊语和意第绪语。

苏斯博士夫妇喜欢在家请客聚会。客人们总是围在钢琴边唱歌。有时夫妻俩还会以特别的方式招待客人，比如乘坐直升机绕加利福尼亚海岸游玩。泰德和朋友们仍喜欢互相搞恶作剧。

出名后，随之而来的各种事情占据了泰德越来越多的时间。仅 1957 年，书迷的来信就重达上千磅。海伦回

复了大部分信件。她署名“苏斯博士夫人”。

泰德仍害怕在公众场合发言，但现在名气这么大，有时难免发言。他发现如果发言稿用韵文的形式来写，他还是能完成发言的。有一次他对一大群书商说：“在场的各位无疑都知道……我完全不会用散文的方式发言。”

第十章

我为大树求情

在与泰德共度了多年的快乐生活后，海伦又病倒了，她还患上了抑郁症。1967 年 10 月 23 日，她去世了，享年六十八岁。四十年来，她事无巨细地照顾泰德。她处理钱财事宜，保护他免受公众打扰，仔细检查他写的每一句话。泰德根本不知道如何独自生活。他需要一个伴侣。1968 年，他娶了奥德丽·迪蒙德，她是盖泽尔夫妇多年的好友。

泰德不介意说初次认识奥

德丽时，她不仅没看过他的书，而且从未听说过苏斯博士的大名。所以他作为“我们尊敬的苏斯博士”被介绍给大家时，她以为他是一个医生[①]。

---

① 苏斯博士（Dr. Seuss），Dr. 也有医生的意思。

不过奥德丽很快就喜欢上了他的书，并和他探讨书里面的每一个细节，正如海伦曾经做的一样。

泰德和奥德丽婚后不久，泰德的父亲去世了，享年八十九岁。多年来泰德一直担心父亲对他很失望。有时很长时间两人都不说话。但随着泰德越来越成功，生活越来越幸福，父子俩也成了好朋友。泰德一直珍惜

父亲给他的那块巨大的恐龙足迹石头。他带着这块石头从一栋房子搬到另一栋房子。

1970 年，泰德塔楼窗户外面的拉霍亚海滨风景变样了。曾经，放眼看去，到处都是海滩和树木，但现在只有各种各样的房子。他决定写一本关爱大自然的书。这是他第一次还没编好故事或选定角色，就先确定了书的主题思想。

泰德说：“写《老雷斯的故事》是我做过的最难的事。当时我阅读了大量事实资料，再加上我十分关心自然世界，以至于把故事写成了一篇讲座。”他完全陷入了写作

僵局，这时奥德丽对他说：“我们去非洲。”

在肯尼亚，泰德惊喜地发现，那里的树木恰好和他为新书虚构的树一模一样——树干细长，顶部有丰满的彩色绒毛。“我的特鲁弗拉树被偷到这里来了！”他大声说。一次观兽之旅中，他看见一群野生象慢悠悠地走过。突然他完全明白了自己想说什么。他拿起几张废纸，几乎一口气写完了整个故事。

《老雷斯的故事》讲述了一片美丽土地的故事，该地生长着特鲁弗拉树。万斯勒想把树都砍掉，运到他的工厂里去用。而老雷斯“替大树求情”。泰德最喜欢他这本书，但最初销量不好。因为大家感觉书里面的内容大部分都是说教。几年后，每个人都树立了环保的意识，阅读此书的人越来越多。

1989 年，《老雷斯的故事》成了苏斯博士第一本面临审查的书。伐木业人士希望此书不被列入学校推荐书目。但是泰德说他并没有反对伐木或者伐木业。“我的住房是木材做的，写的书也被印刷在纸上。”他解释。他只是反对有些人太贪婪而过度伐木，忽视所造成的破坏。

1984 年，《黄油大战》出版。同样，有一些人憎恨此书。此书讲述了尤克人和佐克人之间的故事，两族敌对，不断制造更大、更高端的武器来打击对方，最终都造出了足以让对方顷刻灭亡的武器。两族对峙，不知道接下来会发生什么。泰德觉得自己无法写出一个令人欣慰的欢喜结局。毕竟，真实世界里，美国和苏联都试图制造更大、更厉害的武器。所以在《黄油大战》里，泰德让读者去思考故事应该如何结束。

有些人希望图书馆的书架上不要摆放这本书。泰德曾多番努力说服美国政府加入第二次世界大战。那他怎么会写一本反对战争的书呢？奥德丽宽慰他说：“你不仅为孩子们写书，你也为全人类写书。”这本书的成功足以证明她的观点是正确的。《纽约时报书评》杂志最畅销成人书榜单上，第一次有一本儿童书登榜六个月。

泰德喜欢开玩笑说他要对冷战的结束负责。1990年，《黄油大战》被改编成电视剧在苏联播放。“自那以后，”泰德说，“苏联开始解体。”

第十一章

你要去的地方！

写《黄油大战》的同一年，泰德收获至高荣誉——普利策奖。美国写作界的这个奖项从未颁发给儿童书籍作家。连泰德本人也很惊诧，很久才相信这是真实的，并非一起恶作剧。

1990 年，他出版《你要去的地方！》，书中总结了他的人生观，并用插图总结了他的作品。如果仔细阅读，你能看到书中到处都有他早期作品的一些细节。苏斯博士通过整个故事直接跟读者们对话，他描绘了一个年轻人迈上人生之路后会遇到的所有挑战和冒险。他留下了振奋人心的结尾，但并没有许下承诺："你会成功吗？会，当然会！"

泰德意识到这本书很可能是他写的最后一本书。他快八十六岁了。一生中大部分时候，他是个老烟枪。他总是没办法戒烟，即便被口腔医生诊断出口腔癌，还是没能戒烟。不到两年，1991 年 9 月 24 日，泰德·盖泽尔去世，享年八十七岁。临终时他对妻子说："我一生活得精彩。做了该做的事，过了想过的生活。收获了爱，收获了一切。"

遵照泰德的意愿，不举办丧礼，不立坟，不起碑。但世界各地的人都怀着深深的爱哀悼他，纪念他。在达特茅斯学院，师生们坐在户外二十四小时，一起阅读他的书籍。

尽管泰德·盖泽尔去世了，但是苏斯博士还活着。在他的职业生涯中，他一共写了大约四十本书。2001 年，《出版人周刊》列出最畅销的一百五十本儿童书的清单，

其中二十四本是苏斯博士的作品。

泰德的长期代理商估计，美国四分之一的儿童看的第一本书就是苏斯博士写的。而且《你要去的地方！》这本书是最受高中和大学毕业生欢迎的礼物。时至今日，泰德·盖泽尔诞辰一百多年后，苏斯博士的书仍然贯串了大部分美国人的童年。

西奥多·苏斯·盖泽尔生平年表

1904 年	—	西奥多·苏斯·盖泽尔 3 月 2 日出生。
1921—1925 年	—	在达特茅斯学院学习。
1927 年	—	与海伦·帕尔默结婚。
1928 年	—	开始画“快，亨利，拿‘一扫净’！”广告。
1931 年	—	苏斯博士的插画第一次印刷成书。
1937 年	—	第一本书《桑树街漫游记》出版。
1943 年	—	加入美国陆军电影部门。
1954 年	—	《霍顿与无名氏》出版。
1957 年	—	《戴帽子的猫》和《圣诞怪杰》出版，成为“初级读物”公司总裁。
1960 年	—	《绿鸡蛋和火腿》出版。
1966 年	—	《圣诞怪杰》登上电视。
1968 年	—	娶奥德丽·迪蒙德。
1984 年	—	荣获普利策儿童文学特别贡献奖。
1991 年	—	9 月 24 日，苏斯博士去世。

世界大事记

1903 年 — 美国开始修建巴拿马运河。
1914 年 — 第一次世界大战爆发。
1918 年 — 第一次世界大战结束。
1920 年 — 美国实施禁酒令。
1929 年 — 经济大萧条开始。
1933 年 — 美国废除禁酒令。
1937 年 — 达菲鸭第一次在电影《猪小弟猎鸭记》中亮相。
1939 年 — 第二次世界大战爆发。
1945 年 — 第二次世界大战结束。
1954 年 — 布朗诉托皮卡教育委员会案结束了美国学校里的种族隔离制度。
1957 年 — 苏联发射人造卫星 1 号和 2 号。
1964 年 — 美国通过民权法案。
1969 年 — 美国阿波罗 11 号完成第一次载人登月任务。
1975 年 — 微软公司成立。
1991 年 — 苏联解体。

Who Was Dr. Seuss?

In 1985, Princeton University awarded honorary degrees to six people. An honorary degree is given to a person who has done something important for the world. The students were most excited about one of the people being honored. When a tall, thin man with a gray beard stood up, they all leaped to their feet. "I am Sam," they chanted. "Sam-I-am." Then they recited, from memory, all of *Green Eggs and Ham*. It was a special way to show Theodor Geisel, better known as Dr. Seuss, how much his books meant to them.

Among the Princeton students that year was Michelle Robinson. Many years later, she married Barack Obama and became the First Lady of the United States. In 2010 she chose another Dr. Seuss book, *The Cat in the Hat*, to read aloud to the nation's schoolchildren. The First Lady knew that books for beginning readers used to be solemn and boring. Then Dr. Seuss appeared with his bouncy rhymes and wild and crazy characters like the Cat in the Hat, Horton, and the Grinch. Learning to read was never the same again.

Chapter 1

Goofy Machines

Theodor Seuss Geisel was born in Springfield, Massachusetts, on March 2, 1904. Springfield was full of factories turning out cars, guns, bicycles, tires, and toys. One of the factories was a brewery that Ted's grandfather had started called Kalmbach and Geisel. Ted's father became the president of the company. Its beer was so popular that the people of Springfield nicknamed the business "Come Back and Guzzle."

Ted grew up in a family that loved wordplay. His mother's family owned a bakery. As a child, she made up rhymes listing the pie flavors. Later, she sang her children to sleep with the same rhymes. Ted believed that his love of verse came from his memories of those pie poems.

His sister, two years older, was named Margaretha. But she nicknamed herself "Marnie Mecca Ding Ding Guy."

His father, also named Theodor, liked to dream up goofy, complicated inventions in his spare time. Ted's favorite was a "Silk-Stocking-Back-Seam-Wrong-Detecting Mirror."

Young Ted loved to hang around the zoo. He got special treatment because his father helped run the zoo. Sometimes, he said, "they'd let me in the cage with the small lions and the small tigers, and I got chewed up every once in a while." (He was famous for exaggerating when he told stories.)

After a visit to the zoo, Ted would rush home and draw animals on the walls of his room. Somehow the animals never ended up looking quite like what he had seen, so he would make up names for them. One of his mother's favorites was a creature with ears that were nine feet long. He called it a Wynnmph.

Like many people in Springfield, the Geisels came from Germany. Ted grew up speaking both German and English. In 1914, World War I started in Europe. Many countries were fighting against Germany. The United States was not in the war yet. (That didn't happen until 1917.) But Germans were becoming very unpopular in America.

At school, German American children were often bullied. Sometimes kids would throw rocks at Ted. The Geisel family tried hard to prove that they were patriotic Americans. Ted' s Boy Scout troop had a contest to see who could sell the most Liberty bonds—a way to help the government support the war effort. Ted's grandfather bought one thousand dollars worth. This made Ted one of the winners.

At the awards ceremony, medals were given out by former president Theodore Roosevelt. But someone in the Boy Scouts had made a mistake. There were ten winners, yet Roosevelt had only nine medals. When he ran out of medals,

Ted was left standing alone onstage. Roosevelt bellowed, "What's this little boy doing here?" No one explained that Ted was a winner, too. Ted slunk away.

From then on, it was very hard for Ted to get up in front of people. Even after he was famous, he refused to give speeches. When he tried to appear on a television talk show, he was so scared that he couldn't say a word.

After the war ended in 1918, Ted's family faced a new problem. As 1920 began, Prohibition became the law in the United States. Prohibition meant that it was illegal to make or sell alcohol—including beer. The brewery had to close, and Ted's father was out of a job. The family still had enough to live on. But the loss of the brewery was a terrible blow. Now the family had much less money, just as Ted was about to graduate from high school. But education was important to the Geisel family. No matter what, they made sure there was enough money for Ted to go to college.

Ted had never paid much attention to his schoolwork.

He spent most of his time writing jokes for the school paper. The one class that interested him was English.

Ted's English teacher had gone to Dartmouth College in New Hampshire. He loved Dartmouth so much that Ted decided to go there, too.

Prohibition

In 1920 it became illegal to sell or manufacture alcohol in the United States. The Eighteenth Amendment, called Prohibition, was passed by activists who thought drinking liquor was ruining people' s lives. But Prohibition was not very successful. Crime groups such as the Mafia became more powerful by smuggling liquor. Gangsters like Al Capone became folk heroes. Most people kept on drinking, even though it meant they were breaking the law. Many towns had a "speakeasy," a place where you could buy alcoholic drinks if you knew the secret password or knock.

The amendment was especially hard on people like the Geisels who had made their living selling alcohol. (Ted never forgot what it did to his family. Many of his early cartoons made fun of Prohibition.) Cities that had been famous for their breweries suddenly lost their most important businesses—and all the tax money and jobs that went with them. Some breweries tried to survive by selling soda. Other places sold grape juice or malt syrup. They included careful instructions telling their customers exactly what not to do to their juice or syrup to make sure it didn't turn into alcohol. By the 1930s, it was clear that Prohibition was a failed experiment. In 1933, President Franklin Roosevelt signed a law that helped end it. Then he said, "I think this would be a good time for a beer."

Chapter 2

A Very Fine Flying Cow

Ted loved Dartmouth. It was located in green countryside with beautiful old buildings. He made friends there who he kept for the rest of his life. Shortly after he arrived, he discovered the school humor magazine, *Jack- O- Lantern*, fondly known as *Jacko*. It became his dream to work on *Jacko*, and he started spending all his time in the office. Staff members would find him there in the morning, fast asleep at his typewriter.

He was quickly elected to the staff and, at the end of his junior year, he was made editor in chief. The students loved his stories and drawings, and he became a very important person at Dartmouth. Even so, his classmates voted him

"Least Likely to Succeed." Ted never seemed to be serious about anything.

A month before graduation, Ted threw a party. The guests shared a bottle of gin. When a couple of boys began horsing around on the roof, Ted's landlord called the police. Because of Prohibition, gin was illegal, so Ted was in a lot of trouble.

As punishment, he was not allowed to write for *Jacko* anymore. But he found a way around this. He signed his work with fake names. He had already used joke names such as Oo-La-La McCarty and Theo LeSieg (LeSieg was Geisel spelled backward). Now he started using just his middle name, Seuss.

At Dartmouth, Ted had spent all his time on *Jacko*. His grades were not very good. Ted's father was afraid that he wouldn't be able to get a job after college. But Ted told his dad not to worry. He was going to Oxford, a famous university in England. What's more, he said, he had won a prize to pay for it! His father was so thrilled that he told the local newspaper. The next day, Ted was headline news.

But there was a problem. Ted *had* applied to Oxford. But he hadn't really won any money. He only hoped he would. Ted had to tell his father the truth. The older Geisel was a very proud man. He had already announced to the world that Ted was going to Oxford. So he decided that he would have to pay for his son to go. In the summer of 1925, Ted boarded a steamship for the long journey to England.

Ted never really fit in at Oxford. The university was about eight hundred years old. All the students seemed very serious. The lectures bored him. Ted tried to listen and take notes, but his mind wandered. Instead, he doodled. The pages of his notebooks were filled with chickens with windmill tails, dogs walking across tightropes, and cows with wings.

Helen Palmer, another American, was at Oxford studying to be a teacher. One day she looked over Ted's shoulder to see what he was drawing.

"That's a very fine flying cow!" she said.

Helen told Ted his drawings were special. She said he should be an illustrator. Helen's remark changed Ted's life. He realized he didn't want to teach. He didn't want to write novels. He just wanted to keep drawing his mixed-up animals. After that, Ted and Helen spent all their time together. One day, he proposed and Helen accepted. But they couldn't get married yet. They didn't have any money.

After she graduated from Oxford, Helen took a teaching job in New Jersey. Ted dropped out of school and moved back in with his parents in Springfield, MA. He knew what he wanted to do with his life. Now he just had to figure out how to make a living from his drawings.

Chapter 3

Boids and Beasties

Back at his parents' house, Ted spent his time drawing cartoons and writing funny articles. He sent them to everyone he could think of—magazines in New York, college friends, advertising agencies. But no one except Helen seemed to be interested in flying cows and dancing dogs.

Then a famous magazine, the *Saturday Evening Post*, accepted a cartoon. Ted had drawn two elegant tourists with parasols. They were sitting on tame camels and imagining that they were brave explorers. He signed it, simply, "Seuss."

The *Post* paid him twenty-five dollars. Even in 1927, that wasn't a lot of money. But it would pay for a month's rent. Ted decided it was enough to show he could earn a living as an illustrator. He moved to New York City. But until he had a steady income, he still couldn't marry Helen. Instead Ted shared an apartment with a friend from Dartmouth. It was cheap and dirty. Every night before they went to bed, they had to take canes and whack away the rats.

Ted's roommate knew someone who worked for a humor magazine called *Judge*. He introduced Ted, and the magazine offered him a job. He would be a writer and artist and earn a salary.

Now he and Helen could marry. They had to change the date of their wedding once because Ted's sister, Marnie, was about to give birth. Ted wanted his whole family to be able to come to his wedding. Ted's niece, Peggy, was born on November 1, 1927. On November 29, Ted and Helen were married in her parents' parlor.

Ted became very popular at *Judge*. He started writing a column called "Boids and Beasties," where he could introduce all his strange, playful creatures. He signed the column, "Dr. Seuss." He added the "Dr." because he had disappointed his father by dropping out of Oxford.

Unfortunately, *Judge* magazine was having money troubles. They didn't always have enough cash to pay their staff. Companies paid for ads in *Judge* with samples of their products instead of money. These samples got passed on to the staff as their salaries. Often Ted was paid in cases of shaving cream or soda. Once he received 1872 nail clippers. That wasn't much help in paying the costs of everyday life.

Then, in 1928, he had a stroke of luck. It started with Flit, a popular bug killer. Before air-conditioning, people had to leave their windows open in the summer to let in cool breezes. Houses became full of bugs. Ted started thinking about how awful summer must have been for the knights of old. It was bad enough having bugs inside—what if dragons could fly in and bite you?

He drew a cartoon showing a knight in armor who can't get to sleep because there is a dragon in his room. The caption says: “Darn it all, another dragon. And just after I’d sprayed the whole castle with Flit.”

The wife of an advertising executive for Flit was at a beauty salon where she happened to see the cartoon in a magazine. She loved it so much, she made her husband hire Ted to do all the Flit ads.

Ted drew people in funny situations being attacked by huge bugs. This became one of the most successful advertising campaigns in history.

Today, few people remember the tagline Ted invented: “Quick, Henry, the Flit!” But from the late twenties to the fifties, *everyone* knew it. Comedians quoted it, and it appeared in popular songs. Sales of Flit shot way up. And Dr. Seuss’s drawings became famous.

Flit hired Ted at a salary of twelve thousand dollars a year—a lot of money at the time. The next year, the stock market crashed, and America plunged into the Great Depression. All over the country, people were out of work, poor, and starving. But thanks to Flit, Ted had plenty of money.

With his new wealth, he and Helen began throwing parties. They had a very active social life, and Ted became famous in their circle of friends for his practical jokes. Once he sneaked into the kitchen and put a huge plastic pearl in one of the oysters that was going to be served at dinner. Another time, he filled a friend's bathtub with Jell-O and goldfish.

In 1931, Ted's mother died at the age of fifty-two. Her early death was a shock to Ted. But at least she had lived long enough to see his first big success.

Flit made Ted financially secure for life, but there was one problem: He didn't want to spend all his time drawing Flit ads. But his contract wouldn't let him do most other kinds of work. Years later he wrote, "I would like to say I went into children's book work because of my great understanding of children." But it wasn't really true. Actually, illustrating children's books was one of the few things his contract let him do.

New York Apartments

The Geisels' first apartment in Manhattan was right across the street from a horse stable. Soon they moved to a better apartment. Their new phone number was only one digit different from a nearby fish store. They often got telephone calls from people who wanted to buy fish. Instead of telling them they had the wrong number, Ted would draw a picture of the fish they had ordered and deliver it. Not everyone was amused at the time, but just think what those drawings would be worth today!

Chapter 4

What I Saw on Mulberry Street

An editor at Viking Books saw the Flit advertisements and hired Ted to illustrate a book of mistakes made by schoolchildren. So Ted found himself drawing pictures for silly quotations like, "Benjamin Franklin produced electricity by rubbing cats backward." The book was published in 1931. To Ted's surprise, it became a big hit—and Viking signed him up to do a sequel.

Ted soon realized he'd make more money if he wrote and illustrated his own books. He began looking for the perfect subject for his first book.

In 1936, Ted and Helen took a trip to Europe. On the ship ride home, he scribbled picture book ideas in his notebook—

ideas like "a stupid horse and wagon" and "flying cat pulling Viking ship." Nothing seemed quite right. Meanwhile, the throbbing noise of the ship's engines was driving him crazy. He started fitting words to it. Suddenly he found himself chanting, "And *that* is a *story* that *no* one can *beat*. And to *think* that I *saw* it on *Mulberry Street*."

And there was his story. A little boy walking home on Mulberry Street—a main street in Ted's hometown—looks for something interesting to tell his father about. All he can see is "a plain horse and wagon." But by the time he reaches his house, he has turned the horse and wagon into a whole circus parade, with blue elephants and a brass band.

All the rhymes in Dr. Seuss's books bounce along so naturally that people think they must have been easy to write. But Ted worked hard. "I know my stuff looks like it was all rattled off in twenty-eight seconds," he complained, "but every word is a struggle." For one picture book, he might write and tear up five hundred or even one thousand pages.

Finally Ted was happy with *And to Think That I Saw It on Mulberry Street*. He started sending it to publishers. They all rejected it. Most editors found it just too different. They thought the verse was rough and silly. Worst of all, it didn't have a moral. It wouldn't help make children behave better. "What's wrong with kids having fun reading without being preached at?" Ted yelled.

Ted was about to give up when he ran into another Dartmouth friend. Marshall McClintock had just that day become the children' s book editor for Vanguard Press. Vanguard often published books that were "different." They were delighted with the book and immediately said yes. Ted was so grateful, he named the hero in the book "Marco" after McClintock's son.

Chapter 5

An Elephant up a Tree

Reviewers loved *Mulberry Street*, and it sold very well—for a children's book. But during the Depression, people didn't have a lot of money to spend on children's books. To make a living, Ted had to keep doing ads. He said he couldn't tell if he was a real author or "just a lowly advertising man."

His second book was inspired by one of his favorite things—hats. He and Helen liked to travel. Everywhere they went, he would buy hats—maybe a fireman's hat from Peru or a fancy European helmet. Sometimes when he got stuck while writing, he would put on a hat as a "thinking cap." One day Ted would invent the most famous hat of all and put it on a cat, but for now, he wrote *The 500 Hats of Bartholomew Cubbins*.

Ted and Helen had recently learned they could not have children. Later, Ted said he hadn't wanted kids, anyway. They made him nervous. "You have 'em, I'll amuse 'em," he would tell people. But his niece believed that, really, he would have loved to have had a child.

He dealt with the sad news in his own way. He invented a daughter named Chrysanthemum-Pearl and dedicated his new book to her. He and Helen sometimes included Chrysanthemum-Pearl on their Christmas cards, along with other imaginary children such as Norval, Wickersham, and Thnud.

With two children's books out, the name of Dr. Seuss was becoming well-known. Ted had always pronounced his name in the German fashion: "Zoyce." But most of his readers said "Soose." Ted liked that this rhymed with *Mother Goose*, so he started saying "Soose," too.

Random House, a much bigger publisher than Vanguard, became interested in Dr. Seuss. The head of Random House, Bennett Cerf, promised to publish anything Ted wrote. How could he resist? He was sad to leave his friends at Vanguard. But he loved Random House. They stayed his publisher for the rest of his life. Over the years, he became close friends with many of the people he worked with there.

His first book for them was not what Random House hoped for. *The Seven Lady Godivas* was for grown-ups and was full of pictures of naked ladies. This was not Ted's strong point, and Bennett Cerf didn't think the book was very good. Still he kept his promise to let Ted publish whatever he wanted. The book was a complete flop. Ted went back to children's books.

One day around 1939 (at least as he told the story), Ted left his window open. The wind blew around some doodles he had left out. When he came back, there was a drawing of an elephant on top of a drawing of a tree. Why would an elephant be in a tree? Was he hatching an egg? Ted named the elephant Horton, but he got stuck trying to figure out what should happen to him.

"I'm very upset," Helen told a friend, "because Ted has that elephant up a tree, and he doesn't know how he's going to get him down." It was Helen who finally came up with an ending. Horton would hatch an elephant-bird—like the flying cow she had once seen doodled in Ted's notebook.

Ted loved *Horton Hatches the Egg* more than anything else he'd written. He told his editor that it was the funniest children's book ever. Everyone else loved it, too. Horton the elephant is still one of Dr. Seuss's most beloved characters.

But by the time the book came out in 1940, Ted was not thinking about elephant-birds. He was worried and unhappy about what was going on in the world around him. World War II had broken out in Europe. His parents' homeland, Germany, was now controlled by Adolf Hitler and the Nazis. Hitler wanted to rule all of Europe. Most Americans still hoped the United States could stay out of the war, but not Ted. Even though he hated war, the Nazis had to be stopped. If his funny drawings could convince people to buy Flit, could they convince them to fight Hitler? Ted turned his attention to the war and did not write another children's book for seven years.

Chapter 6

Private SNAFU

Ted began drawing political cartoons that criticized people who thought America should stay out of the war. He showed them as ostriches burying their heads in the sand, ignoring the danger around them.

On December 7, 1941, Germany's ally, Japan, bombed Pearl Harbor in Hawaii, and the United States entered the war. Now Ted felt that just drawing cartoons wasn't enough. At thirty-seven, he was old to be a soldier, but he enlisted in the army, anyway. The army knew exactly what to do with a gentle, clumsy artist who couldn't shoot a gun. He was sent to Hollywood, California. There he made movies to train new soldiers.

Ted didn't know anything about making movies, but he knew how to hold people's interest. He helped create the Private SNAFU cartoons. Private SNAFU was a lazy, careless soldier who did everything wrong. (SNAFU stands for "Situation Normal, All Fouled Up.") Private SNAFU showed soldiers what *not* to do.

Later, Ted was promoted to working on live films. He helped write two films about what the US should do in Germany and Japan after the war was won. Revised versions of the films both won Oscars. But today they are completely unknown.

With two Oscars to his credit, Ted thought maybe he would work on movies instead of books. But he quickly changed his mind. He saw that the postwar world would be full of promise as well as danger. He decided nothing was more important than writing children's books. "The new generations *must* grow up to be more intelligent than *ours*," he wrote.

The Question of War

At the beginning of 1941, eighty percent of Americans were against the idea of the United States joining the war against Germany. With an entire ocean separating America from Europe, these people—called isolationists—felt that the troubles in Europe were very far away. They believed that the duty of the United States was to protect itself.

But Ted did not feel isolated from the fighting in Europe. He said, "While Paris was being occupied by the clanking tanks of the Nazis . . . I found I could no longer keep my mind on drawing pictures of Horton the elephant." In his political cartoons, Ted tried to show how closely the countries of the world were connected to one another. In one drawing, he showed Uncle Sam happily taking a bath. Uncle Sam is thinking, "The old family bathtub is plenty safe for me." Because his eyes are shut, he does not see that the tub is filled with a shark, a crocodile, and a poisonous bug ready to chomp on him.

Chapter 7

A Moose, a nerd, and the Whos

Ted's joy at the end of World War II was cut short by the death of his sister, Marnie. Because of a family quarrel, she and Ted had fallen out of touch. She died before they could make up. Her death upset him so much that he avoided talking about her for the rest of his life.

Now that the war was over, Ted and Helen decided to stay in California. They bought an old observation tower on a mountain outside La Jolla, a beautiful California town on the Pacific coast. For years, the tower had been empty, and it was a favorite meeting place for young couples. The walls were covered with carved initials. Even after the Geisels moved in, some couples would still try to come inside.

One of Ted's first books after the war was *Thidwick the Big-Hearted Moose*. Thidwick is too nice and lets other animals push him around. At the end of the story, Ted asks readers, "Well, what would YOU do if it happened to YOU?" Ted ended many of his books this way, by asking questions. He wanted kids to enjoy his stories. But he also wanted to help them think for themselves.

Ted began to turn out one or two books every year. They were funny, original, and very different from one another. People often asked Ted where he got his ideas. He said that he usually started by doodling. "I may doodle a couple of animals. If they bite each other, it's going to be a good book." After a while he got tired of this question. He started saying that he got his ideas from the people in a small town "called Über Gletch. I go there on the fourth of August every summer to get my cuckoo clock repaired." From then on, he gave this answer to everyone—even President John F. Kennedy's wife, Jacqueline.

Some of his books were inspired by the real world. In 1953, *Life* magazine sent Ted and Helen to Japan to find out how the country was coping after the war. Ted had mixed feelings about the Japanese. In his wartime cartoons, he had shown Japanese people—even US citizens—as villains.

But as he talked to teachers and schoolchildren in Japan, he got past this prejudice. He saw that the people of Japan were trying to honor the importance of each individual and still work together for the common good.

Back in his studio, Ted explored what he had learned in Japan. To do this, he returned to one of his most beloved characters—Horton the elephant. In *Horton Hears a Who!*, Horton must save the tiny world of Who-ville by proving it exists. He can do this only by getting every Who, even the very smallest and laziest, to work together. Horton is willing to risk everything for the Whos because "a person's a person no matter how small." Ted dedicated the book to a Japanese friend.

By the time *Horton Hears a Who!* was published, personal troubles had taken over Ted' s life. Helen was suffering from a terrible illness. She could not breathe on her own and had to be put in an iron lung—a huge metal case that enclosed most of her body. Ted spent hours sitting beside her in the hospital. When she came home, Ted rigged up mirrors so Helen could watch their dog playing outside.

Ted had relied on Helen for everything. She helped him with all his books and ran his life for him. Without her, he didn't even know how to balance a checkbook.

Helen amazed her doctors by recovering almost completely. By May 1955, she was able to travel back to Dartmouth with Ted to see him get an honorary doctorate. Years ago, he had disappointed his father by not earning a degree from Oxford. But now he made up for it. He was no longer just Dr. Seuss, he boasted. He was *Dr.* Dr. Seuss.

The First Nerd

Ted loved to invent words like *thneed and Sala-ma-goo*. One of his words escaped from its book and became part of the English language. Dr. Seuss was the first person to use the word *nerd.* In *If I Ran the Zoo*, published in 1959, young Gerald McGrew plans to "sail to Ka-Troo and bring back... a NERD." No one knows quite how it happened, but within a year, teenagers in Detroit were using *nerd* to mean " a drip or square," and soon the new word had spread across the whole country.

Chapter 8

The Cat in the Hat Arrives

In 1954, an article appeared in *Life*, a popular weekly magazine. It asked why American children had so much trouble learning to read. Was it because books for beginning readers were so boring? Teachers thought children learned to read by seeing the same words over and over. So early readers used short, choppy sentences that just kept repeating the same thing. Why would smart children read these dull books? If someone like Dr. Seuss wrote an early reader, maybe children would actually want to read it.

A friend of Ted's, William Spaulding, worked for the publisher Houghton Mifflin. He read the article and said to Ted, "Write me a story that first-graders can't put down!"

Ted was willing to try. Random House and Houghton Mifflin worked out an agreement. Houghton Mifflin would sell the book to schools and libraries, and Random House would sell it to bookstores.

William Spaulding gave Ted a list of about three hundred words that most first-graders should know. The book could only use about 225 words, and all of them had to come from this list. Ted thought it would be easy to toss off a little story—but he soon found out it was almost impossible. Every time he had an idea, he needed a word that wasn't on the list. He spent more than a year trying and failing. Finally he decided, "I'll read (the list) once more and if I can find two words that rhyme, that will be my book." He found them—*cat* and *hat*—and *The Cat in the Hat* was born.

The Cat in the Hat was published in 1957. Many teachers didn't like it. They thought it looked too much like a comic book and it wasn't serious. Some librarians hid it and hoped kids wouldn't find it. Houghton Mifflin, which handled school and library sales, didn't sell many copies.

But kids loved *The Cat in the Hat.* They read it and told their friends about it. Bookstores couldn't keep it on the shelves. It just kept selling and never stopped. Within three years, it had sold over one million copies. Of everything he had ever written, Ted said, "It's the book I'm proudest of . . ."

At Random House, Bennett Cerf's wife, Phyllis, thought *The Cat in the Hat* should be just the beginning. She wanted to publish a whole series of books like it—books that used just a few words but were so much fun kids would actually want to read them. She convinced her husband to let her start a new company at Random House. It would be run by Phyllis, Ted, and Helen. Called Beginner Books, it would publish beginning readers by Dr. Seuss and also by other people.

Right away, Beginner Books was a hit. Random House became the nation's largest publisher of children's books. Ted was happy to publish books by old friends from his army days, like P. D. Eastman, who wrote *Are You My Mother?* and *Go, Dog. Go!* He also published a book by Marshall McClintock, the Vanguard editor who had given him his start years before. And he discovered books about a family of bears written by Stan and Jan Berenstain.

Bennett Cerf was amused by the word list Beginner Books authors had to use. If writing a book using only three hundred words was so hard, he asked, what about one with even fewer? He bet Ted fifty dollars that he couldn't write a book using only fifty words. Bennett Cerf lost his bet. Ted wrote and illustrated *Green Eggs and Ham* using exactly fifty words. It remains the most popular of all his books and the fourth best-selling children's book of all time.

The Baby Boom

Beginner Books began at the best possible time. After World War II, American families started having lots of children. By 1957, there were more kids just learning to read than ever before. At the same time, the United States was more and more afraid of the USSR, a group of Communist countries. People were worried that schools in these countries were better at training children to become scientists and inventors. So in 1958, the US government began to pour money into schools and libraries. Some of this money was used to buy books like Dr. Seuss's Beginner Books series.

Chapter 9

Grinches and Turtles and Sneetches

In 1957 *The Cat in the Hat* turned Ted into a superstar author. He had become the head of his own publishing house. As if that wasn't enough for one year, he also invented the Grinch.

Ted liked to hint that the Grinch was Dr. Seuss himself. He even had a license plate that said "GRINCH." As for where the name came from, he said, "I just drew him and looked at him, and it was obvious to me who he was."

As soon as it was published, *How the Grinch Stole Christmas!* was a big hit. A few years later, Ted got a call from an old friend, Chuck Jones. He was now a famous animator, and the creator of Road Runner and Wile E. Coyote. He wanted to make a version of the Grinch for TV. Ted was uneasy about the idea, but he trusted Jones. He even let him turn the Grinch green. (He had been black-and-white with pink eyes in the book.) The Grinch Christmas special appeared on TV in 1966 and has been a holiday favorite ever since.

Ted and Helen finally had exactly the life they wanted. They had plenty of money, so Ted didn't have to do any more ads. Helen was happy to take care of all the practical details of life so he could just write and draw all day. They did not have family of their own, but they became close with Ted's niece, Peggy.

Ted had loved playing with Peggy when she was a baby. Even after he and Marnie were not speaking, he kept in touch with Peggy. In her twenties, Peggy moved out to California. She lived in the Geisel's tower for a while. She even got married there. Her son, another Ted, named Teddy, was like a grandson to the Geisels. He was quiet and gentle like Ted, and he wanted to be an artist. Teddy was one of the few people Ted would allow into the studio while he was working.

Over the next ten years, Ted wrote twelve books, including classics like *The Cat in the Hat Comes Back, One Fish Two Fish Red Fish Blue Fish,* and *Hop on Pop!*

All of Ted's stories were a lot of fun, but they also brought up serious ideas. *Yertle the Turtle and Other Stories* is about a tyrant who pushes everyone around and an ordinary little turtle who is brave enough to stand up to him. Ted based *Yertle* on Hitler, and he worried that people might object to this. But actually, the only problem came when the little turtle burps. "Nobody had ever burped before on the pages of a children's book," Ted explained.

Another book that meant a lot to him was *The Sneetches and Other Stories*. During the early 1960s, black people were struggling to win their civil rights. In his book, Ted described all the trouble between the star-bellied Sneetches and the Sneetches without stars. The story shows how silly Ted thought it was for people to hate one another because they looked different.

It was hard work writing all those books. Ted spent eight hours a day at his desk, seven days a week. He said that he did his best work when he wrote himself into a corner—"so there was seemingly no way of ending the book"—and then had to write his way out.

Helen had to deal with Ted's moods while he was doing this. She explained, "About two weeks before the completion of every book he . . . decides that nothing in the book is any good . . ." Then she had to talk him out of throwing the whole thing away.

After he finished a book, he was just as bad. He would worry, "I'm never going to write anything, I've lost it, I just can't do it." Then one of his doodles would start his mind moving, and he'd be happy again.

Work was always the center of Ted's life. But sometimes he did take a break. He and Helen enjoyed traveling all over

How Do You Say Grinch in Chinese?

At first, Dr. Seuss's books were not well- known outside the United States. People in England thought they were too "American"—vulgar, rude, and slangy. And it was hard to introduce the books to other countries because Dr. Seuss's rhymes and invented words were almost impossible to translate. Clever translators tried, however, and soon Dr. Seuss' s fame spread around the whole world. Eventually his books appeared in more than twenty languages, including Chinese, Swedish, Spanish, Hebrew, Maori, Latin, Japanese, Greek, and Yiddish.

the world. They looked at elephant seals in Mexico. In Peru, they helped search for mummies. They went to Australia, Africa, and Hawaii.

At home, they loved to entertain. Guests would gather around the piano and sing. Sometimes the Geisels set up special treats, like a helicopter ride around the California coast. And Ted and his friends still loved to play practical jokes on one another.

The business of being famous took up more and more of Ted's time. In 1957 alone, he received almost a thousand pounds of fan mail. Helen answered most of it. She signed her letters "Mrs. Dr. Seuss."

Ted was still terrified of speaking in public, but now that he was so famous, sometimes he had to. He found that he could do it as long as the speech was in verse. He once explained to a big group of booksellers: "As everyone present undoubtedly knows . . . I am completely incapable of speaking in prose."

Chapter 10

I Speak for the Trees

After many happy years together, Helen began struggling with illness and depression again. On October 23, 1967, she died. She was sixty-eight years old. For forty years, she had taken care of everything for Ted. She handled money matters, shielded him from publicity, and went over every line he wrote. He did not know how to live life alone. He needed a companion. In 1968, he married Audrey Dimond, a close friend of the Geisels for many years.

Ted enjoyed pointing out that when he first met Audrey, not only had she never read any of his books, she had never heard of Dr. Seuss. When he was introduced—as "our very own dear Dr. Seuss"—she assumed he was a medical doctor.

Audrey quickly became interested in his work, however, and soon she was discussing every detail with him, just as Helen had done.

Shortly after Ted and Audrey were married, Ted's father died at the age of eighty-nine. For years Ted had worried that he was a disappointment to his father. Sometimes they did not speak to each other for a long time. But as Ted became more successful and happy with his life, they had become good friends. Ted always treasured the enormous stone dinosaur footprint his father had given him. He carried it with him from house to house all his life.

By 1970, the view of La Jolla from Ted's tower window had changed. Once he had looked out on beaches and trees, but now the land was covered with houses. He decided he had to write a book about caring for the natural world. For the first time, the message for his book came to him before the story or characters.

Writing *The Lorax*, Ted said, was "the hardest thing I

have ever done." He had read so many facts, and he cared so much about the natural world, that the story kept turning into a lecture. When he was completely stuck, Audrey said to him, "Let's go to Africa."

In Kenya, Ted was excited to discover trees that looked just like the puffy ones he had invented for his new book. "They've stolen my truffula trees!" he exclaimed. On a safari trip, he saw a herd of wild elephants ambling by. Suddenly he knew exactly what he wanted to say. He grabbed some scrap paper and wrote almost the whole story in one sitting.

The Lorax tells the story of a beautiful land where truffula trees grow. The Once-ler wants to chop them all down to use in his factories. It is the Lorax who "speaks for the trees." It was Ted's favorite of all his books, but it didn't sell very well at first. People thought it preached too much. A few years later, when saving the environment was on everyone's mind, the book found its audience.

In 1989, *The Lorax* became the first Dr. Seuss book to

encounter censorship. The logging industry wanted it off school reading lists. But Ted argued that he wasn't against logging or industry. "I live in a house made of wood and write books printed on paper," he pointed out. He was just against the greed that made people go too far and ignore the damage they caused.

In 1984, *The Butter Battle Book* came out. It, too, made some people angry. It tells the story of the Yooks and the Zooks, enemies who keep building bigger and more complicated weapons to fight against each other. Finally they each have a weapon that could destroy everyone. They stand facing each other, wondering what will happen next. Ted didn't feel he could write a comforting happy ending. After all, in the real world, the United States and the USSR were both trying to build bigger, better weapons. So in *The Butter Battle Book*, Ted left it up to his readers to think about how the story should end.

Some people wanted this book taken off of library

shelves. Ted had worked hard to convince the United States to fight in World War II. How could he write a book against war? Audrey comforted him by telling him, "You're not just writing books for children, you're writing for humanity." The book's success proved her point. It was the first children's book ever to spend six months on the adult best seller list of the *New York Times Book Review*.

Ted liked to joke that he was responsible for the end of the Cold War. In 1990, a version of *The Butter Battle Book* was televised in the Soviet Union. "Right after that," Ted pointed out, "the USSR began falling apart."

Chapter 11

Oh, the Places You'll Go!

The same year he wrote *The Butter Battle Book*, Ted received a great honor—a Pulitzer Prize. This prize for American writing had never been given to a children's book writer. He was so surprised that he had a hard time convincing himself it wasn't a hoax.

In 1990, he published *Oh, the Places You'll Go!*, summing up his view of life. The illustrations sum up his work, too. If you look carefully, there are details from his earlier books everywhere. Dr. Seuss speaks to his readers directly throughout the whole story, describing all the challenges and adventures facing a young person starting out on the road of life. He ends cheerfully, but he doesn't make any promises:

"And will you succeed? Yes, you will indeed! "

Ted realized this book would probably be his last. He was almost eighty-six years old. For most of his life, he had been a heavy smoker. He was never able to break the habit, even after his dentist found cancer in his mouth. Less than two years later, on September 24, 1991, Ted Geisel died at the age of eighty-seven. One of the last things he told his wife was, "I've had a wonderful life. I've done what I had to do. I lived where I wished to live. I had love. I had everything."

As Ted had wanted, he had no funeral and no grave. But people everywhere mourned him and remembered him with love. At Dartmouth, the students and teachers sat outside for twenty-four hours reading his books aloud.

Even after Ted Geisel's death, Dr. Seuss lived on. During the course of his career, he wrote some forty books. In 2001, when *Publishers Weekly* drew up a list of the top 150 best-selling children's books of all time, twenty-four were by Dr. Seuss.

Ted's longtime agent estimated that something by Dr. Seuss is the first book given to one out of every four children born in the United States. And *Oh, the Places You'll Go!* is one of the most popular gifts for high school and college graduates. So today, over a century after Theodor Geisel was born, most American childhoods begin and end with Dr. Seuss.

Timeline of Theodor Seuss Geisel's Life

1904	Theodor Seuss Geisel born on March 2.
1921-1925	Attends Dartmouth College.
1927	Marries Helen Palmer.
1928	Begins drawing "Quick, Henry, the Flit!" advertisements.
1931	Dr. Seuss illustrations appear in a book for the first time.
1937	Publishes his first book, *And to Think That I Saw It on Mulberry Street.*
1943	Joins the United States Army Motion Picture Unit.
1954	Publishes *Horton Hears a Who*!
1957	Publishes *The Cat in the Hat and How the Grinch Stole Christmas!* and becomes president of Beginner Books.
1960	Publishes *Green Eggs and Ham.*
1966	*How the Grinch Stole Christmas!* appears on TV.
1968	Marries Audrey Dimond.
1984	Wins special Pulitzer Prize for contribution to children's literature.
1991	Dr. Seuss dies on September 24.

Timeline of the World

1903	The United States begins work on the Panama Canal.
1914	World War I begins.
1918	World War I ends.
1920	Prohibition begins in the United States.
1929	Beginning of the Great Depression.
1933	Prohibition repealed.
1937	First appearance of Daffy Duck, in a Looney Tunes film.
1939	World War II begins.
1945	World War II ends.
1954	Brown v. Board of Education of Topeka makes racial segregation of schools illegal in the United States.
1957	Soviet Union launches *Sputnik 1* and *2.*
1964	United States Civil Rights Act is passed.
1969	United States' *Apollo 11* is the first manned mission to land on the moon.
1975	Microsoft is founded.
1991	Soviet Union collapses.

Bibliography

* Cohen, Charles D. The Seuss, the Whole Seuss, and Nothing but the Seuss: A Visual Biography of Theodor Seuss Geisel. Random House Books for Young Readers, New York, 2004.

Morgan, Judith, and Neil Morgan. Dr. Seuss and Mr. Geisel: A Biography. Random House, New York, 1995.

Nel, Philip. Dr. Seuss: American Icon. The Continuum International Publishing Group, Inc., New York, 2004.

Pease, Donald E. Theodor Seuss Geisel. Oxford University Press, New York, 2010.

* Seuss, Dr. Your Favorite Seuss: A Bakers's Dozen by the One and Only Dr. Seuss. Compiled by Janet Schulman and Cathy Goldsmith. Random House Books for Young Readers, New York, 2004.

*Starred books are for young readers.